THE GOLDEN BOOK OF
RHODES
THE CITY OF THE KNIGHTS

Text by
VASSILIA PETSA-TZOUNAKOU

Consultant
MICHAEL ARFARAS

BONECHI

Publication created and designed by Casa Editrice Bonechi
Graphic design and photographic research by Serena de Leonardis
Graphics and layout by Maria Rosanna Malagrinò
Editing by Rita Bianucci
Text and captions by Vassilia Petsa-Tzounakou
Consultant: Michael Arfaras
Translation by Vassilia Petsa-Tzounakou
Drawings by Stefano Benini

Photographs from the Archives of Casa Editrice Bonechi
taken by Paolo Giambone *and* Andrea Pistolesi.
The photograph on page 5 is by Gianni Dagli Orti.

INTRODUCTION

GEOGRAPHY - HISTORY

Rhodes, the largest island in the Greek Dodecanese, is situated in the southeast of the Aegean, opposite the intricately winding south shoreline of Asia Minor. According to myth, the island took its name from Rhode, a sea nymph, daughter of Aphrodite and wife of the Sun God Helios. Home of great athletes in antiquity, Rhodes was praised by Pindar in his 7th Olympionicus, written in 464 B.C. to celebrate the Olympic victories of Diagoras of Rhodes.

Pottery, stone utensils and tools of bone, flint and obsidian prove the existence of widespread human presence in neolithic times. Most of the sites already explored are along or near the wind-protected southeast coast. Minoan and Mycenaean civilization spread from Ialyssos and Kamiros, on the northwest coast.

Myth and archaeological evidence agree as to the arrival of an Achaean tribe from Argolid in the 15th century B.C. A Bronze Age settlement was established at the site of ancient Ialyssos, on Mt. Phileremos. In the next three centuries, pottery of a Rhodian Mycenean type reached other Mediterranean lands due to flourishing commerce. During the Dorian invasion at the end of the 12th century B.C., Heracleides Tlepolemos and his people settled on Ialyssos, Kamiros and Lindos. In 700 B.C., the Doric Hexapolis was founded by the above three Rhodian cities, Cos, Cnidus and Halicarnassus; the Sanctuary of Apollo Triopios in Cnidus was their seat. In the 7th century B.C., Rhodians built colonies in Asia Minor, Magna Grecia, on the Mediterranean coast of contemporary France and on the Valearids. At the same time they dominated the goods trade in the east Mediterranean.

Ancient Rhodes had a strong economy and a naval force. It therefore was a target for military and economic alliance or subjugation. In 491/490 B.C., Darius I of Persia dispatched strong military and naval forces which, nevertheless, failed to subjugate the island. In 480 B.C. however, Rhodians reinforced the Persian fleet in the sea battle at Salamis. They subsequently joined the First Athenian Confederacy in 478/477 B.C., after the defeat of the Persians. Aiming to best serve the interests of his homeland, Rhodian leader Dorieus withdrew from the Athenian Confederacy during the Peloponnesian War. He sided with the Spartans and supported their fleet against the Athenians in the sea-battle at Symi, in 412/411 B.C.

The island's fame was to be further promoted, when settlers from Ialyssos, Kamiros and Lindos jointly founded the city of Rhodes in 408 B.C., on an orthogonal grid plan, in the Hippodameian manner.

The Rhodians established friendly relations with Alexander the Great when it had become clear that the Macedonians had won supremacy over the Persians. They also forged good trade connections in Alexandria, Egypt. When one of Alexander's successors demanded that the Rhodians turn against Egypt, he received a refusal. As a consequence, Demetrios Poliorketes attacked Rhodes. His year-long siege ended with a settlement.

During the era of the Roman expansion in the Mediterranean, Rhodes was both a considerable ally and an opponent of the Romans. The Rhodian admiral Eudamos defeated Hannibal, the formidable enemy of the Romans, at the sea-battle in Side, Pamphylia, in 190 B.C.. However, Rhodian sovereignty in Caria and Lycia on the coast of Asia Minor was lost to the Romans in 167 B.C.. An agreement was reached between the Rhodians and the Romans in 164 B.C., making an obligation for mutual alliance. At the same time, prominent Romans began to arrive in Rhodes to receive instruction by philosophers and orators. Rhodians supported Roman ranks during the Third Carthaginian War (167 B.C.) and in the Mithridatic Wars (88-63 B.C.). As the island supported Julius Caesar in the Civil War, it was subsequently besieged, captured and plundered by Cassius in 42 B.C. In the years that followed, Rhodes lost its naval power and its destiny was determined by the will of the Roman emperors. After the fierce raids by the Goths, a Germanic tribe, in A.D. 263-269, Diocletian united Rhodes with the Roman Province of the Islands and made it its capital at the end of the third century A.D.

Little is known about the history of Rhodes in the Early Christian years. The island was temporarily seized from the Byzantines by the Persian King Chosroes II, in A.D. 620. The parts of the bronze Colossus of Rhodes, which had lain on the ground since the destructive earthquakes of 225 B.C., were sold by Arabs under the Chaliph Muawiyah in 653 B.C. The Byzantine fleet launched attacks against the Saracen pirates from Rhodes in A.D. 718. A fleet led by Harun Al Rashid, Chaliph of the Baghdad Abbasids, raided Rhodes in A.D. 807. During the Third Crusade, Richard the Lionheart of England and Philip II of France came to Rhodes and recruited mercenaries. Byzantine nobleman, Leo Gavalas, ruled Rhodes from 1204-1240. After his death, the island was officially under Byzantine command; however, in reality, it was under the control of Genoese admirals.

Knight rule commenced in 1309. From that time, the island became the bone of contention in a struggle for religious supremacy in the Mediterranean. Finally, in 1522, cunning Suleiman the Magnificent, the Ottoman ruler, subjugated Rhodes.

In 1911, Italy declared war against Turkey and Italian forces captured Rhodes in May 1912. The Italian occupation lasted 33 years, until the end of World War II. In May 1945, the Italian Commander of Rhodes was handed over by the Germans to the Allied Forces, who collaborated with the Greek Sacred Regiment to liberate the island. Power was transferred to the Greek admiral Pericles Ioannides by the Provisional British Command on 31 May 1947. The formal union of the Dodecanese with Greece was declared in Rhodes almost a year later.

Page 2: Bronze deer on a pedestal. Entrance to the Mandraki Harbor.

Imaginary drawing of the Colossus of Rhodes according to oral tradition.

ANCIENT RHODIAN LETTERS

*F*rom archaic times, Rhodes rose as an independent hub of Hellenic intellectualism. It gradually became a pole of attraction for intellectuals from other lands. Leading savants, like Athenian rhetorician Aeschines, settled on the island. Rhodians who had studied abroad returned to Rhodes, like peripatetic philosopher Eudemus, who had been a student of Aristoteles.

Apollonius Rhodius, third century B.C. poet and philosopher, was actually born in Alexandria or Naucratis in Egypt. In Rhodes, he revised his much acclaimed epic poem Argonautica and produced so much intellectual work that he was given the cognomen Rhodius.

Intellectual activity in Rhodes manifested itself in a multitude of disciplines: philosophy, oratory, historiography, poetry and epigram, medicine, geography, astronomy and mathematics. Many savants occupied themselves with more than one discipline. Important astronomic observations and some of the first geographic measurements were made in Rhodes.

SAMPLES OF ANCIENT RHODIAN ART

*M*onumental works of painting and sculpture were exhibited in public places. They bore witness to the flourishing civilization and the sturdy economy of the island. Paintings by classical painter Parrhasius of Ephesus were on display in Rhodes and in Lindos. Works by Apelles, the official painter of the Macedonian court, were to be found in Rhodes, just as was a colossal four-horse bronze chariot by Lyssipus, Alexander's favorite portrait sculptor.

The Colossus of Rhodes (ca. 300 B.C.), bronze statue of the Sun God Helios measuring 31 meters, was made by sculptor Chares of Lindos. It was considered one of the Seven Wonders of the Ancient World. According to oral tradition, it stood astride the harbor entrance and ships passed underneath.

The Winged Victory of Samothrace, now in the Louvre, and the bronze Sleeping Cupid in the Metropolitan Museum of Art in New York, are attributed to Rhodian Hellenistic workshops. The statue of the Victory was probably a Rhodian offering to the Sanctuary of the Great Gods in Samothrace.

A monumental Rhodian sculpture group of the Roman era showed the sons of Antiope punishing Dirce by tying her onto the horns of a raging bull. It is known in ancient literature and from a Roman copy, Taurus Farnese, in the National Museum of Naples, Italy.

The walled city and its environs, and the ports of the City of Rhodes. Illustration from a 16th century book of sailing directions in the Old Library of St. Mark's, Venice.

RHODES
THE CITY OF THE KNIGHTS

Left page: South entrance. Palace of the Grand Master.

The Palace of the Grand Master and part of the city fortifications. Northeast seaward view.

HISTORY OF THE CITY OF THE KNIGHTS

A great part of the island of Rhodes was ceded against payment to the Knights of the Order of St. John of Jerusalem by Genoese admiral Vignolo da Vignoli in 1306. By 1309, the Knights had gradually conquered the entire island. In the 213 years of their stay in Rhodes, they undertook considerable building work; in the Old Town of Rhodes, which is still called City of the Knights, they left indelible samples of their architecture. The city walls and the buildings of the Knights were restored by the Italians in the early 20th century and they are now preserved by the Greek State.

The medieval town was surrounded by an external wall and a moat. It was divided into two unequal, al-most rectangular parts by an internal wall. Greeks, western laymen and Jews inhabited Chora, the largest part of the Old Town, in the south. The Knights lived in the smallest of the two parts, known as Castello or Collachium, to the north. In this part were the Palace of the Grand Master, the Inns and the Hospital of the Knights. The members of the Order were divided into Tongues, according to their place of origin. Each Tongue was housed in its own building or Inn, where officials and guests of the Order lived and where the Knights dined.

Western thought and the centuries-long local Byzantine tradition mingled in the cultural life of Rhodes during the era of the Knights. Greek and

Western scholars and artists gathered in the court of the Grand Masters. In the second half of the 15th century, the Greeks regained the right to have their own Orthodox Metropolitan under the Pope, and they renovated or built new churches and monasteries. Life in Rhodes at the end of the 15th century was described by the Greek poet of that time Emmanuel Georgillas Limenites.

The main concern of the Knights was the repulsion of Islam. An Egyptian fleet besieged Rhodes in 1440 and 1444 but it was turned back both times. The Ottoman Turks set up two major sieges forcing the Knights to bolster their fortifications and to spend a good part of their financial resources. Grand Master Pierre d'Aubusson warded off the danger in 1480. In a diplomatic move, in 1482 he granted asylum to Prince Djem, who lay claim to the Turkish throne. In remembrance of the victory in 1480, the erection of Our Lady of the Victory was started in Gothic style in the southeast corner of Chora; the church was never completed. In 1522, following a siege and treaty, Rhodes was handed over to the Ottomans. The Knights and 4,000 Rhodians left for Crete. Marking a new era in the town's history, Suleiman the Magnificent prayed for the first time in the Byzantine church of Haghia Aikaterini, which was converted into a mosque called Ilk Mihrab or First Prayer Niche.

Left page. Top: The remains of Naillac Tower and the cylindrical Trébuc Tower.
Bottom: The Palace of the Grand Master.

Plan of the City of the Knights. From left to right, the coats of arms of England, Navarre, Portugal, Germany, France-Auvergne, Provence and Castille-Aragon; below, the coat of arms of the Maritime Republics.

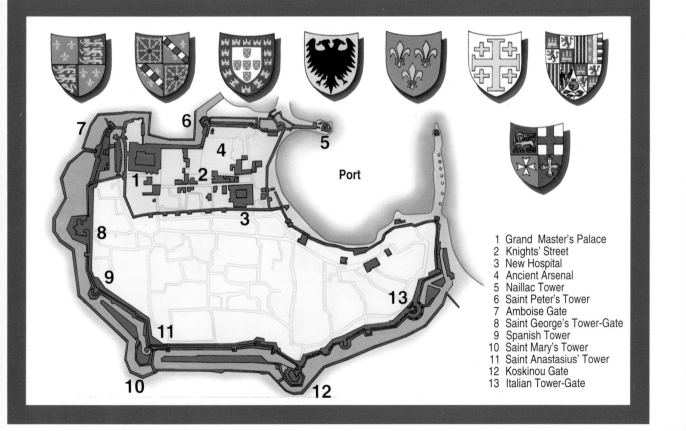

1 Grand Master's Palace
2 Knights' Street
3 New Hospital
4 Ancient Arsenal
5 Naillac Tower
6 Saint Peter's Tower
7 Amboise Gate
8 Saint George's Tower-Gate
9 Spanish Tower
10 Saint Mary's Tower
11 Saint Anastasius' Tower
12 Koskinou Gate
13 Italian Tower-Gate

Left page: The moat, the advance wall and a rectangular defensive tower on the curtain wall.

The Gate of Liberty (1924) links the Old with the New Town.

A VISIT TO THE CITY
OF THE KNIGHTS

Plateia Symis is accessible from the Gate of Liberty on the north walls, and from Arsenal Gate. The Municipal Gallery is housed in a 15th century reconstructed building in the square and contains fine samples of 20th century Greek painting and works by folk painter Theophilos. In adjacent Argyrokastrou Square, the Inn of the Tongue of Auvergne (1507) has three arches on the ground floor facade and an upstairs loggia. In the same square, the Old Hospital of the Knights had also been used as an armory; it now houses the Greek Archaeological Service. Like other buildings dating from the first building phase of the Knights, it has a plain facade. The main entrance was later constructed in the inte-

rior of the apse of the Hospital's Gothic chapel.
Our Lady of the Castle (11th century) is situated opposite the entrance to the Street of the Knights. Its choir apse lies next to the walls and culminates in a tower without defensive function; the tower merely contributed to the visual adaptation of the building to the architecture of the walls. Initially the seat of the Orthodox Metropolitan, the church had an inscribed-cross plan with a dome. In the first building phase of the Knights, it became the seat of the Catholic Archbishop. The interior of the church was remodelled into three aisles and a transept. Gothic ribbed groin-vaults were added to the ceiling, pointed arches and stained glass to the windows. During

The Street of the Knights. View of the north side.

Right page. Top and bottom right: The Inn of the Tongue of France. First floor detail and view of the facade respectively. The ornamental mouldings and window frames, the gargoyles, the semicylindrical turrets and the false crenellations add distinctive grace to the facade. Together in the square frame are the coats of arms of France and of Pierre d'Aubusson. Below is the coat of arms of Philippe de l'Isle Adam. Bottom left: The Inn of the Tongue of Italy. Detail of the facade with the coat of arms of Fabrizio del Carretto framed by an ogive pointed arch.

THE STREET OF THE KNIGHTS

One of the most beautiful medieval streets, the cobbled Street of the Knights, starts from the Church of Our Lady of the Castle, at the edge of Museum Square, and culminates in the entrance square of the Palace of the Grand Master. Most of the structures in this street belong to the second building phase, after the Turkish siege of the town in 1480. They are made of well-hewn, isodomically arranged local sandstone. They are distinguished by their fine Gothic decoration of sculpted door and window frames and of horizontal mouldings, which make a pleasant contrast to the otherwise plain surface of the wall. The Inns of the Knights were two-storeyed and bore on the facades the coats of arms of the Order and of the officials who had played an important role in their erection, extension or repair. Behind the Renaissance-like arcades of the ground floor, there were storage rooms and an interior courtyard. The main entrance was on one side of the facade and stairs led to the rooms on the first floor.

17

Top left: The Chapel of France. Detail of the facade with a statue of the Madonna and Child in a Gothic canopied niche. Top right: The north side of the street showing the same Chapel and, next to it, the House of the Prior of France. The arched passageway nearest to the picture plane belongs to the Inn of Spain on the south side of the street and joins it to the Inn of Provence. Bottom: The arch at the top of the Street of the Knights.

Left page: The Inn of the Tongue of Provence. Main entrance. The coats of arms are of the Order, of France, of Fabrizio del Carretto and of the Prior of Toulouse F. Flotta.

The Palace of the Grand Master. South view.

Next page. The inner courtyard. Top: View from the east.
Bottom: The north loggia and the niches with the statues
of the Roman emperors.

THE PALACE
OF THE GRAND MASTER

The Palace of the Grand Master is situated in the northwest corner of the walls, in the highest part of the Collachium. It was the fortified residence of the highest official and the administrative center of the Order. Its construction started soon after the arrival of the Knights in Rhodes, on the remains of the 7th century Byzantine Acropolis. It suffered great damage in 1856, during the Turkish rule, with the explosion of ammunition stored in the church of the patron saint of the Order, St. John of the Collachium, south of the palace. When the Italian Cesare Maria de Vecchi was Commander of the Dodecanese, a radical reconstruction took place in 1937-40, so that the building could be used as a summer residence by the Italian high officials of that time. The role of the Palace as a decision-making center was renewed in December 1988, when its rooms were used during the European Summit Meeting.

The Palace is built around the perimeter of an inner courtyard measuring 50x40 meters. Situated in its south side, the main entrance is flanked by two horseshoe-shaped tall towers, reminiscent of those of the Marine Gate, which is the town's impressive entrance point from the sea. In the center of the inner coutyard, there are wells and, in niches along its north side, statues of Roman emperors from the early 20th century Italian excavations at the Odeum in Cos. Shady stoas border the south and the east

side of the courtyard on the ground floor. An external stair on the east side leads a to northerly loggia on the first floor.

The Chapel is halfway up the stair from the covered entrance passageway to the first floor of the Palace. It contains a bronze copy of Donatello's St. Nicholas and marble relief depictions of scenes from the life of Christ and the Saints by early 20th century Italian sculptor Montoleone.

The rooms of the Palace were decorated with mosaics and statues from Cos and with functional and decorative objects of Western European and Oriental art of the 16th-19th centuries. A copy of the Laocoon group is also on display at the Palace. The first century B.C. original by Rhodian sculptors Agesander, Athenodorus and Polydorus is now in the Vatican Museum.

Top and next page, bottom: Views of the hypostyle hall with the Hellenistic trophy and Late Roman and Early Christian mosaic floors from the island of Cos. Reused granite columns with Early Christian capitals support the freely reconstructed row of arches. During the era of the Grand Masters, the Palace was decorated with carved wooden furniture, carpets, tapestries and precious vases. Bottom: The broad, vaulted, marble staircase leading to the first floor of the Palace.

Next page. Top: Within a square frame, an apotropaic head of the Gorgon Medusa with motifs radiating out from the center of the composition. Mosaic of the Late Hellenistic era. The art of the mosaic spread to Cos and Rhodes from the 3rd century B.C. depicting themes from mythology, geometric and naturalistic compositions.

Top: View of a room with ribbed groin-vaults and Renaissance wooden pews. The windows of the Palace afford magnificent views of the city and the sea. Bottom: Copy of the Laocoon group. Like the Taurus Farnese, another sculptural group of the Roman era, the Laocoon depicts a favorite theme of that time, namely human agony in combat with uncontrolled natural forces.

Next page. Mosaics from Cos made with quadrangular pieces of stone. Top: Sea Horse and Numph, 1st century B.C. Bottom: Gladiator and Tiger, Hellenistic period.

Left page. Another room in the Palace with a ceiling of timber and a freely reconstructed row of arches. On the floor is a 5th century A.D. mosaic with an elaborate geometric composition from the Early Christian basilica of Haghios Johannes in Cos. In the wall niches are 17th century wooden candleholders in the shape of angels. The masonry of the reception rooms of the Palace is plain, with isodomically arranged local sandstone. Wall paintings adorn rooms on the ground floor, on the mezzanine and in the residential quarters.

Top: Room of the mosaic with the Nine Muses. Over the fireplace is the grandiose coat of arms of the Italian dynasty.
Bottom: Late Hellenistic mosaic depicting the heads of the Nine Muses and their attributes, set in medallions.

The Hospital of the Knights. Bottom: View of the inner courtyard of the Hospital showing the two-storeyed, arched facade.

Next page. Top: Late Hellenistic lion holding a bull's head in its front paws. Made of local grey marble. Bottom: View of the inner courtyard of the Hospital.

THE ARCHAEOLOGICAL MUSEUM OF RHODES

The Archaeological Museum of Rhodes is housed in the Hospital of the Knights. Its construction started in 1440 but it was completed during the second building phase of the Knights.

The seven ground floor arches on Museum Square led to storage rooms. The Chapel of the Hospital was on the first floor over the main entrance with the Gothic portal. Architecturally, the Hospital reflects the eastern tradition of buildings such as Byzantine hospices and oriental caravanserais, which developed around a central courtyard in one or two arched storeys.

Some of the Museum's exhibits are presented in the next pages. Separate mention must be made of the silver coins of the ancient city of Rhodes. On one face, they bore the head of the Sun God Helios. On the other was a rose in relief with an inscription of the coin's origin.

Top: The funerary stele of Kalliarista from a cemetery in the city of Rhodes, dedicated by the deceased woman's husband, Damocles. First half of 4th century B.C. Bottom left: The funerary stele of Krito and Timarista from a cemetery in Kamiros, showing a tender last farewell. End of 5th century B.C. Bottom right: The Aphrodite of Rhodes (1st century B.C.).

Left page. Top: View of the archaic sculpture room. Head and torsoes of Kouroi (550-520 B.C.), found in Kamiros. Bottom left: Marble head of the Sun God Helios (2nd century B.C.). Bottom right: Fragment of a female funerary statue. Second half of 4th century B.C.

Top: View of a room in the Museum with a Late Hellenistic statue of Aphrodite of the Arles type. Bottom: Three-sided Archaistic Late Hellenistic sculpture found on the Acropolis of Rhodes. It contains three sculpted images of the Goddess Hecate of the Underworld. The goddess wears an archaic chiton in the manner of the Athenian Korae and bears a cylindrical headdress and a three-legged caldron on her head.

Next page. View of the Museum garden with Hellenistic and Roman exhibits.
Bottom left: Dolphins from a funerary monument, made of grey marble. Middle of 2nd century B.C.
Bottom right: Mosaic floor from the Early Christian basilica of Arkasa in Karpathos (6th century A.D.), now in the sunken courtyard of the Museum garden.

33

Top left: Archaic clay idol connected with the cult of Demeter and Persephone. Top right: Attic olpae, or wine vessel, with Dionysian themes.
Bottom: Black-figured amphora (6th century B.C.) with banded decoration. Human figures, wild animals and mythological monsters are depicted in formal compositions.

Top: Attic olpae, or wine vessel,
with Dionysian themes.
Bottom left: Rhodian oinochoe,
7th century B.C. Bottom right:
Attic oinochoe in the shape
of a female head.
First half of 5th century B.C.

36

The infirmary ward of the Hospital of the Knights. It now contains coats of arms and funerary reliefs from the era of the Knights. The Chapel was in the apse with a flamboyant Gothic arch, on the longer side of the room, over the Hospital's main entrance. The coats of arms of the Order and of Grand Master Pierre d'Aubusson can be seen at the point where the arches meet the columns.

Right page: Archaic clay female head. First half of 5th century B.C.

Views of the Museum interior. On the left, a Dodecanesian 'pataros', which is an elevated sleeping area sheltered by a screen carved in wood.

THE MUSEUM OF POPULAR ART

The Museum of Popular Art is in Argyrokastrou Square. One of its highlights is the Rhodian sperveri, a silk-embroidered curtain which adorned the nuptial bed. The Museum also contains a great variety of ceramic plates which were originally made in Asia Minor; they are known as Rhodian or Lindian plates because their production spread on the island, too. They date from the 16th-18th centuries and depict boats and a variety of motifs from the plant and animal world. Local costumes, multicolored embroidery, painted wooden chests, wood carved furniture, decorative objects and items of everyday use provide a colorful picture of art and tradition in the Dodecanese.

Ippokratous Square. View of the southeast side.

THE CITY
WITHIN THE WALLS

Churches, public buildings, shops and houses were to be found within the city walls in the era of the Knights. During the Turkish rule, which lasted approximately four centuries, the Greeks were obliged to leave Chora and to settle in areas outside the walls. The churches were converted into sites of Muslim worship and six new mosques were constructed in central locations.

There are 24 well-known Byzantine churches in the Old Town. They date from the Christian era in the history of the city which lasted about 13 centuries, including the rule of the Knights. They can be classified into five architectural types. Fifteenth century Haghios Georghios, with its elegant elevated dome,

is the only one with a quatrefoil plan. As an architectural type, it derives its plan from concentric buildings such as the Roman mausolea and the Early Christian martyria. A Franciscan monastery was housed in Haghios Georghios during the rule of the Knights. During the Turkish occupation, a Muslim theological seminary was founded there. It is known as Chourmali Medrese, or the School at the Date Palm. Haghios Georghios is located near the Bastion of St. George, on the west side of the walls. Three fresco-painting styles can be distinguished in the Byzantine churches on the island of Rhodes: the Byzantine, the West European and the eclectic, or mixed style. In the Old Town, thirteenth century

Castellania (1507). An Aegean-type external staircase leads to the first floor balcony. A marble relief lintel in Renaissance style can be seen on the left. The ground floor arcade and the horizontal arrangement of the facade are also Renaissance traits. The coat of arms of Grand Master Emery d'Amboise is set in a flamboyant Gothic frame.

Next page. Top: View of the Marine Gate from Ippokratous Square. Bottom: Our Lady of the Burgum (ca. 1400). Pointed choir apses.

Haghios Phanourios on Dorieus Square has a free-cross plan with a dome and contains well preserved 13th-15th century frescoes in the Byzantine style. A fresco dating from 1335-1336 depicts the donors and two children. In the southwest part of the Old Town, Haghia Aikaterini, or Ilk Mihrab, is a three-aisled, vaulted church with an irregular plan made up of three trapezoids due to the location where it was erected. It contains 14th-15th century frescoes also executed in the Byzantine style. On the inner face of the western wall, over the entrance, is a fresco depicting Christ and the donors.

In the southwest part of the Old Town, Haghios Nikolaos has gothic architectural elements and frescoes of mixed Byzantine and West European style, dating from the era of the Knights. Haghia Triada,

or Dolapli Mesjid (14th-15th century), a Byzantine church with a free-cross plan and a dome, is situated in the southeast part of the Old Town and also contains mixed West European and Byzantine style frescoes. A baptistery or narthex added to the north arm of the cross had a pointed octagonal dome over squinches of an Islamic type.

A remarkable sample of dominant Western influence is a fragment of a fresco in Our Lady of the Castle, depicting Santa Lucia in the Tuscan 14th century manner.

Saint John of the Collachium, Our Lady of the Burgum and Our Lady of the Victory had a Gothic character from the start.

The Muslim Library was founded in 1794 by the Rhodian Muslim Ahmed Chaphouz Aga. It was ini-

tially housed in the Mosque of Murad Reis, outside the city walls. It is now in a building opposite the Mosque of Suleiman and contains Turkish, Arabian and Persian manuscripts, some of which are illuminated, and an anonymous chronicle of the siege in 1522.

The Synagogue was founded in the center of the Jewish quarters in the 16th or 17th century although the Jewish community in Rhodes is considerably older. In the same area, the Hospice of St. Cather-

Top: The 19th century Clock Tower near the Mosque of Suleiman. Bottom: The Mosque of Suleiman, rebuilt in 1808. A Renaissance marble arcosolium from an important funerary monument of the era of the Knights has been reused as a door frame in this mosque.

Left page: Top left: The House of the Greek Orthodox Metropolitan on the Square of the Jewish Martyrs is identified by Latin and Greek inscriptions on the building. It dates from the second building phase of the Knights and is characterized by Renaissance symmetry and horizontal aspect. The fountain with the sea horses was constructed by the Italians in the early 20th century. Top right: The Mosque of Suleiman from the east. Bottom: Views of Sokratous Street.

ine, founded by Fra Domenico d'Alemagna, was renovated in 1516 by Costanzo Operti. It provided shelter to Italian Knights on pilgrimage to the Holy Land. On the facade are the coats of arms of Operti and of Grand Master Fabrizio del Carretto. There is also a relief of the wheel, the symbol of St. Catherine's martyrdom.

The building of Castellania, the commercial court of the Knights, bears witness to the flourishing economy in Rhodes during that era. Only the southwest part of the building is preserved. It now houses the Public Library of Rhodes and the Historical Archives of the Dodecanese.

Purification fountain and minaret. Mosque of Redjeb Pasha (1588), on Dorieus Square. Architectural pieces from monuments of the Byzantine and Knight eras have been used. The mosque was decorated with Persian faience tiles. Bottom and next page: Characteristic cobbled and paved streets with arched overhead passages and structural supports. Cobbled interior courtyard.

45

Top and bottom: Ippokratous Square, night views. In the picture at the top, the dome of Chandrevan Mosque is outlined in the horizon.

Left page: Top: Recent preservation scaffolding at the Mosque of Sultan Mustafa (1765), on cool Arionos Square. In the architecture of the Mosque, elements from the Christian art of building are combined with the Muslim tradition. The Baths of Mustafa on the same Square are contemporary with the Mosque. Bottom: The Mosque of Ibrahim Pasha (1531), south of Ippokratous Square, is the oldest Islamic sacred edifice in Chora.

THE OLD TOWN AND THE WALLS

At first the Knights found it sufficient to reinforce and repair the 7th and 12th century Byzantine fortifications. From the end of the 14th century, the walls took a new shape. The medieval fortification of the city of Rhodes was based on construction methods brought over by the Knights from their native lands. These methods were influenced by the invention and use of artillery weapons, which was the latest development in the art of warfare. The numerous coats of arms on the walls bear witness to the contribution of the Pope and successive Grand Masters to the repair, maintenance and reinforcement of the walls and the moat.

During the second Turkish siege, each Tongue had undertaken the defense of a particular sector of the walls. The Tongue of Germany had taken over the sector from the Gate d'Amboise, to the west of the Palace, until the Bastion of St. George, along the west line of the walls. In a counterclockwise movement, the Tongue of Auvergne covered a continuous part of the walls until the Tower of Spain. The sector of the Tongue of Spain-Aragon followed, until the Bastion of Our Lady and, along the south side of the walls, the sector of England, until the Bastion of St. John, at Koskinou Gate. The Tongue of Provence had taken over the defense until the Bastion of del Carretto and the Tongue of Italy, the east side, until St. Catherine's gate at the port. The seaward line of the walls was controlled by the Tongue of Castille, while the north sector was occupied by the Tongue of France. The port entrances were guarded by the Fort of France and the Naillac Tower at the entrance to the present day Commercial Harbor, and by the Fort of St. Nicholas, to the north of the medieval town, at the Mandraki harbor entrance. When the Gate d'Amboise (1512) was constructed

The Temple of Aphrodite on Symis Square. Third century B.C., with Roman additions.

Next page. Top: The Gate of Liberty and part of the moat. Bottom: Rectangular defense tower along the west line of the walls.

Marine views at Mandraki. Top: View of the Metropolis of Rhodes with the tall bell tower. In the background are the Shipping Companies' Offices and the Port Authority. Bottom: Tourist vessels anchored at the Mole of St. Nicholas.

Next page. Top: The north and the east side of the Palace of the Grand Master. Behind the anchored vessels is part of the Municipal Garden. Bottom: The New Market with elements of Islamic construction and style. On the facade of the tall entrance gate are coats of arms bearing a cross, which was the characteristic symbol of the Order and, by extension, of the Italian state of occupation and, today, of the city of Rhodes.

Venetian Gothic style with elements of Moorish tradition. The Town Hall, the Law Courts, the Port Authority Building, the Post Office, the National Theater and the Hotel des Roses are built in the austere and imposing style of Italian official architecture of the early 20th century. The New Market is a low polygonal structure around an inner courtyard, in the manner of oriental markets. The Church of the Annunciation, which is now the Metropolis of Rhodes, contains frescoes of Byzantine inspiration

Mandraki. Top: A natural-sponge vendor's stall.
Bottom: Flag masts at the Mole of St. Nicholas.

Next page. Top: Reconstructed medieval mills at Mandraki.
Bottom: The Fort of St. Nicholas (1464-1467).

THE NEW TOWN NEAR THE PORT

The medieval town is surrounded by new quarters to the north, west, and south. During the Italian occupation (1912-1945), some public buildings were constructed to the west of the Mandraki Harbor, on the site of one of the five ports of ancient Rhodes. On the whole, they display a variety of form and style. Although they do not reflect the Aegean style of architecture, they are interesting from a historical point of view. The building of the Prefecture, the former Italian Governor's Palace, is a mixture of

Bastion of St. John, there is a unique marble slab embedded in the wall with a bilingual inscription, in Greek and Italian, dated August 20, 1457. It commemorates the contribution of Greek master mason Manuel Koundes to the fortification works, under the rule of Grand Master Jacques de Milly.

In addition to the Temple of Aphrodite, within the city walls, to the north, was the Sanctuary of Dionysus, which contained important works of art. The Sanctuary of the Sun God Helios must have been at the site of the Palace of the Grand Master; according to recent archaeological research, the Colossus of Rhodes also stood there in antiquity.

The Gate of St. Paul. Top: Cylindrical defense tower. Bottom: The Gate from the west.

Right page: Views of the defense enclosure.

Top: The Gate of Koskinou. Bottom: The Gate of St. Athanassios.

Left page. Top: The Gate d'Amboise. Bottom: Western view of the Palace and the fortifications

on the northwest corner of the walls, it enclosed three older and smaller ones and created an additional fortified enclosure to the west of the Palace. The two low cylindrical towers flanking the Gate had openings at the top for the positioning of artillery weapons. The square tower at the Bastion of St. George was constructed during the third decade of the 15th century. On the western face, it bears a relief depicting St. George killing the dragon, and the coats of arms of Pope Martin V, of the Order and of Grand Master Antoni de Fluviañ. Defense works were completed under the rule of Grand Masters Pierre d'Aubusson and Villiers de l'Isle Adam, when the Islamic threat had reached a climax. At the

by the 20th century Greek painter Photis Kondoglou. It was built during the second decade of the Italian occupation as a copy of St. John of the Collachium, on the basis of drawings by the Belgian Rottiers. The Mosque of Murad Reis was built on the site of the Knight's church of St. Antony and of the cemetery of the common Knights, opposite the National Theater and the Prefecture. The Mosque was dedicated to Suleiman the Magnificent's admiral during the last siege of Rhodes. In the Turkish cemetery next to the Mosque, some prominent Muslims lie buried, such as a Shah of Persia, a Prince of Crimea, and the 18th century poet Mohamed Ahmed Efendi. In the same cemetery is the circular mausoleum of Murad Reis.

Top: A beach near the walls. Bottom: Sailboats anchored near the Fort of St. Nicholas.

Left page. Top: The Metropolis of Rhodes.
Bottom: The Prefecture.

Next pages: Dusk at Mandraki.

Top: A view of the Stadium and the Odeum of Ancient Rhodes. Left: Thick vegetation on the hill to the east of the Sanctuary of Athena Polias and Zeus Polieus.

Next Page: The Sanctuary of Apollo Pythios.

THE ACROPOLIS OF RHODES

The ancient Acropolis of Rhodes was at Haghios Stephanos, an elevation to the northwest of the Old Town. The texts of treaties with other states were kept in the Sanctuary of Athena Polias and Zeus Polieus, the protectors of the town. On the green slope of the hill, to the east of the Sanctuary, were caves devoted to the Nymphs and stoas that were part of the aqueduct. The Sanctuary of Apollo Pythios was next to the Stadium and the Odeum. Reconstruction work was carried out by Italian archaeologists in the early 20th century. The Acropolis was an important center for religion and for intellectual, artistic and athletic activity. The Gymnasium of the ancient city also lay in the vicinity.

CONTENTS

ISBN 88-8029-495-4

* * *